COMMISSION MEMBERS

Thomas H. Kean
CHAIR

Lee H. Hamilton
VICE CHAIR

Richard Ben-Veniste

Bob Kerrey

Fred F. Fielding

John F. Lehman

Jamie S. Gorelick

Timothy J. Roemer

Slade Gorton

James R. Thompson

1

CONTENTS

TRIUMPH
BOOKS
601 South LaSalle Street
Chicago, Illinois 60605

Introduction

It's been three years since terrorists murdered innocent men, women and children in a cowardly sneak attack. The Nation was devastated.

But America is resilient.

She mourned her dead, honored her heroes and rekindled the pride and patriotism in all things that make America great. She went back to work, back to school, back to living life as Americans, but with the same questions on everyone's lips: How did this happen? How could the strongest country in the world be violated by a gang of thugs? Why weren't we warned? What can we do to make sure this never happens again?

There were countless reports, rumors and speculations about how this happened, but nothing that answered the questions of an increasingly restless America who demanded answers.

Finally, in November 2002, the Congress and the President created the National Commission on Terrorist Attacks Upon The United States. Its mandate was clear: Tell the nation the truth about what happened on September 11, 2001.

The Commission reviewed more than 2.5 million pages of documents, interviewed more than 1,200 individuals, including nearly every senior official from the current and previous administrations who could shed any light on the 9/11 tragedy. They held 19 days of hearings and took public testimony from 160 witnesses. The result is a 585-page report entitled *The 9/11 Commission Report*.

The findings of this government investigation are so important to every American, that we decided to publish this ***Special Edition of The 9/11 Commission Report***.

This ***Special Edition*** will help you understand what went wrong, where responsibility lies and what you need to know about future terrorist attacks. The words you are about to read in this ***Special Edition*** are exactly as written by the Commission.

The report is a historical document that gives us an understanding of the past and reveals how such a tragedy could occur, and provides a guideline for our elected officials to follow to assure the American people that this will never happen again.

And to the terrorists of the world it sends a clear, strong message: Never Again, Because We Will Never Forget.

David Pecker
Chairman/CEO
American Media, Inc.

EDITOR'S NOTE:
The *9/11 Commission Report* is a document every American should read. It answers the questions about how this attack happened and could anyone have prevented the tragedy. This special edition is a condensed presentation of the *Commission Report*. Not a single word has been changed.

Preface

The 9/11 Commission holds its final public hearing in June 2004.

We present the narrative of this report and the recommendations that flow from it to the President of the United States, the United States Congress, and the American people for their consideration. Ten Commissioners – five Republicans and five Democrats chosen by elected leaders from our nation's capital at a time of great partisan division – have come together to present this report without dissent.

We have come together with a unity of purpose because our nation demands it. September 11, 2001, was a day of unprecedented shock and suffering in the history of the United States. The nation was unprepared. How did this happen, and how can we avoid such tragedy again? To answer these questions, the Congress and the President created the National Commission on Terrorist Attacks Upon the United States (Public Law 107-306, November 27, 2002).

We have sought to be independent, impartial, thorough, and nonpartisan. From the outset, we have been committed to share as much of our investigation as we can with the American people. To that end, we held 19 days of hearings and took public testimony from 160 witnesses.

Our aim has not been to assign individual blame. Our aim has been to provide the fullest possible account of the events surrounding 9/11 and to identify lessons learned. We learned about an enemy who is sophisticated, patient, disciplined, and lethal.

We learned that the institutions charged with protecting our borders, civil aviation, and national security did not understand how grave this threat could be, and did not adjust their policies, plans, and practices to deter or defeat it. We learned of fault lines within our government – between foreign and domestic intelligence, and between and within agencies.

At the outset of our work, we said we were looking backward in order to look forward. We hope that the terrible losses chronicled in this report

> *The nation was unprepared. How did this happen, and how can we avoid such tragedy again?*

can create something positive – an America that is safer, stronger, and wiser. That September day, we came together as a nation. The test before us is to sustain that unity of purpose and meet the challenges now confronting us.

We need to design a balanced strategy for the long haul, to attack terrorists and prevent their ranks from swelling while at the same time protecting our country against future attacks. We have been forced to think about the way our government is organized. The massive departments and agencies that prevailed in the great struggles of the twentieth century must work together in new ways, so that all the instruments of national power can be combined. Congress needs dramatic change as well to strengthen oversight and focus accountability.

We decided consciously to focus on recommendations we believe to be most important, whose implementation can make the greatest difference. We came into this process with strong opinions about what would work. All of us have had to pause, reflect, and sometimes change our minds as we studied these problems and considered the views of others. We hope our report will encourage our fellow citizens to study, reflect – and act.

Thomas H. Kean, Chair
Lee H. Hamilton, Vice Chair

How The Terrorists Got Aboard The Planes

Hijackers Atta (right) and Alomari (center) are caught on the surveillance camera as they pass through airport security at Portland International Jetport. They were catching a commuter flight to Boston for American Airlines Flight 11.

Tuesday, September 11, 2001, dawned temperate and nearly cloudless in the eastern United States. Millions of men and women readied themselves for work. Some made their way to the Twin Towers, the signature structures of the World Trade Center complex in New York City.

Others went to Arlington, Virginia, to the Pentagon. Across the Potomac River, the United States Congress was back in session. At the other end of Pennsylvania Avenue, people began to line up for a White House tour. In Sarasota, Florida, President George W. Bush went for an early morning run. For those heading to an airport, weather conditions could not have been better for a safe and pleasant journey. Among the travelers were Mohamed Atta and Abdul Aziz al Omari, who arrived at the airport in Portland, Maine.

Airport Security Failed Boston: American 11 And United 175

Atta and Omari boarded a 6:00 A.M. flight from Portland to Boston's Logan International Airport. When he checked in for his flight to Boston, Atta was selected by a computerized prescreening system known as CAPPS (Computer Assisted Passenger Prescreening System), created to identify passengers who should be subject to special security measures. Under security rules in place at the time, the only consequence of Atta's selection by CAPPS was that his checked bags were held off the plane until it was confirmed that he had boarded the aircraft. This did not hinder Atta's plans.

Between 6:45 and 7:40, Atta and Omari, along with Satam al Suqami, Wail al Shehri, and Waleed al Shehri, checked in and boarded American Airlines Flight 11, bound for Los Angeles. The flight was scheduled to depart at 7:45. In another Logan terminal, Shchhi, joined by Fayez Banihammad, Mohand al Shehri, Ahmed al Ghamdi, and Hamza al Ghamdi, checked in for United Airlines Flight 175, also bound for Los Angeles. A couple of Shehhi's colleagues were obviously unused to travel; according to the United ticket agent, they had trouble understanding the standard security questions,

and she had to go over them slowly until they gave the routine, reassuring answers.

Their flight was scheduled to depart at 8:00. None of the checkpoint supervisors recalled the hijackers or reported anything suspicious regarding their screening.

Logan Airport, Boston, Mass.

While Atta had been selected by CAPPS in Portland, three members of his hijacking team – Suqami, Wail al Shehri, and Waleed al Shehri – were selected in Boston. Their selection affected only the handling of their checked bags, not their screening at the checkpoint. All five men cleared the Checkpoint and made their way to the gate for American 11.

Alarms From Metal Detectors Washington Dulles: American 77

Hundreds of miles southwest of Boston, at Dulles International Airport in the Virginia suburbs of Washington, D.C., five more men were preparing to take their early morning flight. At 7:15, a pair of them, Khalid al Mihdhar and Majed Moqed, checked in at the American Airlines ticket counter for Flight 77, bound for Los Angeles. Within the next 20 minutes, they would be followed by Hani Hanjour and two brothers, Nawaf al Hazmi and Salem al Hazmi. Hani Hanjour, Khalid al Mihdhar, and Majed Moqed were flagged by CAPPS. The Hazmi brothers were also selected for extra scrutiny by the airline's customer service representative at the check-in counter. He did so because one of the brothers did not have photo identification nor could he understand English, and because the agent found both of the passengers to be suspicious. The only consequence of their selection was that their checked bags were held off the plane until it was confirmed that they had boarded the aircraft. All five hijackers passed through the Main Terminal's west security screening checkpoint.

The checkpoint featured closed-circuit television that recorded all passengers, including the hijackers, as they were screened. At 7:18, Mihdhar and Moqed entered the security checkpoint.

Both set off the alarm, and they were directed to a second metal detector

Mihdhar and Moqed placed their carry-on bags on the belt of the X-ray machine and proceeded through the first metal detector. Both set off the alarm, and they were directed to a second metal detector. Mihdhar did not trigger the alarm and was permitted through the checkpoint. After Moqed set it off, a screener wanded him. He passed this inspection.

About 20 minutes later, at 7:35, another passenger for Flight 77, Hani Hanjour, placed two carry-on bags on the X-ray belt in the Main Terminal's west checkpoint, and proceeded, without alarm, through the metal detector.

A short time later, Nawaf and Salem al Hazmi entered the same checkpoint. Salem al Hazmi cleared the metal detector and was permitted through; Nawaf al Hazmi set off the alarms for both the first and second metal detectors and was then hand-wanded before being passed. In addition, his over-the-shoulder carry-on bag was swiped by an explosive trace detector and then passed.

Human Security Fails

When the local civil aviation security office of the Federal Aviation Administration (FAA) later investigated these security screening operations, the screeners recalled nothing out of the ordinary. They could not recall that any of the passengers they screened were CAPPS selectees. We asked a screening expert to review the videotape of the hand-wanding, and he found the quality

Washington Dulles International Terminal

of the screener's work to have been "marginal at best." The screener should have "resolved" what set off the alarm; and in the case of both Moqed and Hazmi, it was clear that he did not.

At 7:50, Majed Moqed and Khalid al Mihdhar boarded the flight and were seated in 12A and 12B in coach. Hani Hanjour, assigned to seat 1B first class), soon followed. The Hazmi brothers, sitting in 5E and 5F, joined Hanjour in the first-class cabin.

Newark Liberty International Airport, Newark, N.J.

Newark: United 93

Between 7:03 and 7:39, Saeed al Ghamdi, Ahmed al Nami, Ahmad al Haznawi, and Ziad Jarrah checked in at the United Airlines ticket counter for Flight 93, going to Los Angeles. Two checked bags; two did not. Haznawi was selected by CAPPS. His checked bag was screened for explosives and then loaded on the plane. The four men passed through the security checkpoint.

The FAA interviewed the screeners later; none recalled anything unusual or suspicious. The four men boarded the plane between 7:39 and 7:48. All four had seats in the first-class cabin; their plane had no business-class section. Jarrah was in seat 1B, closest to the cockpit; Nami was in 3C, Ghamdi in 3D, and Haznawi in 6B.

This is the actual security screening of hijackers Hazmi (top) and 2 other hijackers (below) at Washington Dulles International Airport. They all set off alarms because they were carrying knives, but were cleared to board the flight.

They All Got Aboard

The 19 men were aboard four transcontinental flights. They were planning to hijack these planes and turn them into large guided missiles, loaded with up to 11,400 gallons of jet fuel. By 8:00 A.M. on the morning of Tuesday, September 11, 2001, they had defeated all the security layers that America'8s civil aviation security system then had in place to prevent a hijacking

The Hijacking of American 11

Department of Justice identifies hijackers: (from left) Al Suqami, Waleed Alshehri, Wail Alsheri, Alomari, Atta

American Airlines Flight 11 provided nonstop service from Boston to Los Angeles. On September 11, Captain John Ogonowski and First Officer Thomas McGuinness piloted the Boeing 767. It carried its full capacity of nine flight attendants. Eighty-one passengers boarded the flight with them (including the five terrorists).

The plane took off at 7:59. Just before 8:14, it had climbed to 26,000 feet, not quite its initial assigned cruising altitude of 29,000 feet. All communications and flight profile data were normal. American 11 had its last routine communication with the ground when it acknowledged navigational instructions from the FAA's air traffic control

One spoke very little English and one spoke excellent English

(ATC) center in Boston. Sixteen seconds after that transmission, ATC instructed the aircraft's pilots to climb to 35,000 feet. That message and all subsequent attempts to contact the flight were not acknowledged.

From this and other evidence, we believe the hijacking began at 8:14 or shortly thereafter.

Something Is Wrong

Although the Boston Center air traffic controller realized at an early stage that there was something wrong with American 11, he did not immediately interpret the plane's failure to respond as a sign that it had been hijacked. At 8:14, when the flight failed to heed his instruction to climb to 35,000 feet, the controller repeatedly tried to raise the flight. He reached out to the pilot on the emergency frequency. Though there was no response, he kept trying to contact the aircraft.

Reports from two flight attendants in the coach cabin, Betty Ong and Madeline "Amy" Sweeney, tell us most of what we know about how the hijacking happened. As it began, some of the hijackers – most likely Wail al Shehri and Waleed al Shehri, who were seated in row 2 in first class – stabbed the two unarmed flight attendants who would have been preparing for cabin service. We do not know exactly how the hijackers gained access to the cockpit; Ong speculated that they had "jammed their way" in.

John Ogonowski, Dracut, Mass., Captain, Flight 11

Atta – the only terrorist on board trained to fly a jet – would have moved to the cockpit from his business-class seat, possibly accompanied by Omari. As this was happening, passenger Daniel Lewin, who was seated in the row just behind Atta and Omari, was stabbed by one of the hijackers – probably Satam al Suqami, who was seated directly behind Lewin. Lewin had served four years as an officer in the Israeli military. He

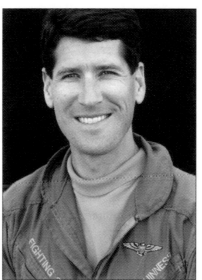

Tom McGuinness, co-pilot, Flight 11

may have made an attempt to stop the hijackers in front of him, not realizing that another was sitting behind him.

Terrorists Take Control

The hijackers quickly gained control and sprayed Mace, pepper spray, or some other irritant in the first-class cabin, in order to force the passengers and flight attendants toward the rear of the plane. They claimed they had a bomb.

About five minutes after the hijacking began, Betty Ong contacted the American Airlines Southeastern Reservations Office in Cary, North Carolina, via an AT&T airphone to report an emergency aboard the flight.

The emergency call lasted approximately 25 minutes, as Ong calmly and professionally relayed information about events taking place aboard the airplane to authorities on the ground. At 8:19, Ong reported: "The cockpit is not answering, somebody's stabbed in business class – and I think there's Mace – that we can't breathe – I don't know, I think we're getting hijacked." She then told of the stabbings of the two flight attendants.

At 8:21, American 11 turned off its transponder, immediately degrading the information available about the aircraft. The controller told his supervisor that he thought something was seriously wrong with the plane, although neither suspected a hijacking.

No Response

At 8:21, one of the American employees receiving Ong's call in North Carolina, Nydia Gonzalez, alerted the American Airlines operations center in Fort Worth, Texas, reaching Craig Marquis, the manager on duty. Marquis soon realized this was an emergency and instructed the airline's dispatcher responsible for the flight to contact the cockpit. At 8:23, the dispatcher tried unsuccessfully to contact the aircraft. Six minutes later, the air traffic control specialist in American's operations center contacted the FAA's Boston Air Traffic Control Center about the flight. The center was already aware of the problem.

Boston Center knew of a problem on the flight in part because just before 8:25 the hijackers had attempted to communicate with the passengers. The microphone was keyed, and immediately one of the hijackers said, "Nobody move. Everything will be okay. If you try to make any moves, you'll endanger yourself and the airplane. Just stay quiet." Air traffic controllers heard the transmission; Ong did not. The hijackers probably did not know how to operate the cockpit radio communication system correctly, and thus inadvertently broadcast their

Madeline Amy Sweeney, Flight Attendant

David Angell, executive producer of *Frasier*, passenger

message over the air traffic control channel instead of the cabin public-address channel. Also at 8:25, and again at 8:29, Amy Sweeney got through to the American Flight Services Office in Boston but was cut off after she reported someone was hurt aboard the flight.

Three minutes later, Sweeney was reconnected to the office and began relaying updates to the manager, Michael Woodward. At 8:26, Ong reported that the plane was "flying erratically." A minute later, Flight 11 turned south.

Sweeney calmly reported on her line that the plane had been hijacked; a man in first class had his throat slashed; two flight attendants had been stabbed – one was seriously hurt and was on oxygen while the other's wounds seemed minor.

At 8:38, Ong told Gonzalez that the plane was flying erratically again. Around this time Sweeney told Woodward that the hijackers were Middle Easterners, naming three of their seat numbers. One spoke very little English and one spoke excellent English.

At 8:41, Sweeney told Woodward that passengers in coach were under the impression that there was a routine medical emergency in first class.

At 8:41, in American's operations center, a colleague told Marquis that the air traffic controllers declared Flight 11 a hijacking and "think he's [American 11] headed toward Kennedy [airport in New York City]. They're moving everybody out of the way. They seem to have him on a primary radar. They seem to think that he is descending."

Boston Center did not follow the protocol in seeking military assistance through the prescribed chain of command. In addition to notifications within the FAA, Boston Center took the initiative, at 8:34, to contact the military through the FAA's Cape Cod facility.

The center also tried to contact a former alert site in Atlantic City, unaware it had been phased out. At 8:37:52, Boston Center reached NEADS. This was the first notification received by the military – at any level – that American 11 had been hijacked:

FAA: Hi. Boston Center TMU [Traffic Management Unit], we have a problem here. We have a hijacked aircraft headed towards New York, and we need you guys to, we need someone to scramble some F-16s or something up there, help us out.
NEADS: Is this real-world or exercise?
FAA: No, this is not an exercise, not a test.

NEADS ordered to battle stations the two F-15 alert aircraft at Otis Air Force Base in Falmouth, Massachusetts, 153 miles away from New York City. The air defense of America began with this call.

'Oh my God we are way too low'

At 8:44, Gonzalez reported losing phone contact with Ong. About this same time Sweeney reported to Woodward, "Something is wrong. We are in a rapid descent ... we are all over the place." Woodward asked Sweeney to look out the window to see if she could determine where they were. Sweeney responded: "We are flying low. We are flying very, very low. We are flying way too low." Seconds later she said, "Oh my God we are way too low." The phone call ended.

F-15 fighters were scrambled at 8:46 from Otis Air Force Base. But NEADS did not know where to send the alert fighter aircraft, and the officer directing the fighters pressed for more information:

"I don't know where I'm scrambling these guys to. I need a direction, a destination." Because the hijackers had turned off the plane's transponder, NEADS personnel spent the next minutes searching their radar scopes for the primary radar return. To avoid New York area air traffic and uncertain about what to do, the fighters were brought down to military airspace to "hold as needed."

American 11 struck the North Tower at 8:46. All on board, along with an unknown number of people in the tower, were killed instantly.

From 9:09 to 9:13, the Otis fighters stayed in this holding pattern.

The Hijacking of American 77

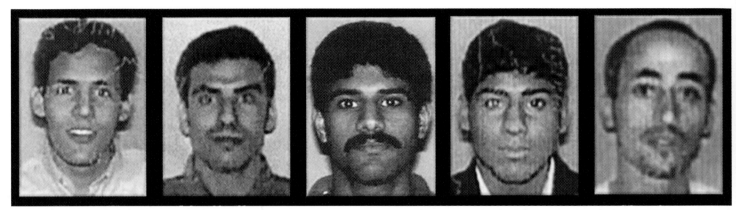

Department of Justice identifies hijackers: Moqed, Almidhar, Nawaf Alhamzi, Salem Alhamzi, Hanjour.

American Airlines Flight 77 was scheduled to depart from Washington Dulles for Los Angeles at 8:10. The aircraft was a Boeing 757 piloted by Captain Charles F. Burlingame and First Officer David Charlebois. There were four flight attendants. On September 11, the flight carried 58 passengers.

At 8:51, American 77 transmitted its last routine radio communication. The hijacking began between 8:51 and 8:54. As on American 11 and United 175, the hijackers used knives (reported by one passenger) and moved all the passengers (and possibly crew) to the rear of the aircraft (reported by one flight attendant and one passenger). Unlike the earlier flights, the Flight 77 hijackers were reported by a passenger to have box cutters. Finally, a passenger reported that an announcement had been made by the "pilot" that the plane had been hijacked.

At 8:54, the aircraft deviated from its assigned course, turning south. Two minutes later the transponder was turned off and even primary radar contact with the aircraft was lost.

Off The Radar Screen

The controller tracking American 77 told us he noticed the aircraft turning to the southwest, and then saw the data disappear. At this point, the Indianapolis controller had no knowledge of the situation in New York. He did not know that other aircraft had been hijacked. He believed American 77 had experienced serious electrical or mechanical failure, or both, and was gone.

Shortly after 9:00, Indianapolis Center started notifying other agencies that American 77 was missing and had possibly crashed.

By 9:20, Indianapolis Center learned that there were other hijacked aircraft, and began to doubt its initial assumption that American 77 had crashed. A discussion of this concern between the manager at Indianapolis and the Command Center in Herndon prompted it to notify some FAA field facilities that American 77 was lost. By 9:21, the Command Center, some FAA field facilities, and American Airlines had started to search for American 77. They feared it had been hijacked. At 9:25, the Command Center advised FAA headquarters of the situation.

In sum, Indianapolis Center never saw Flight 77 turn around. By the time it reappeared in primary radar coverage, controllers had either stopped looking for the aircraft because they thought it had crashed or were looking toward the west. Although the Command Center learned Flight 77 was missing, neither it nor FAA headquarters issued an all points bulletin to surrounding centers to search for primary radar targets. American 77 traveled undetected for 36 minutes on a course heading due east for Washington, D.C.

Telephone Calls From The Aircraft

At 9:12, Renee May called her mother, Nancy May, in Las Vegas. She said her flight was being hijacked by six individuals who had moved them to the rear of the plane. She asked her mother to alert American Airlines. Nancy May and her husband promptly did so.

At some point between 9:16 and 9:26, Barbara

American 77 was missing and had possibly crashed

Olson called her husband, Ted Olson, the solicitor general of the United States. She reported that the flight had been hijacked, and the hijackers had knives and box cutters. She further indicated that the hijackers were not aware of her phone call, and that they had put all the passengers in the back of the plane. About a minute into the conversation, the call was cut off. Solicitor General Olson tried unsuccessfully to reach Attorney General John Ashcroft.

By 9:25, FAA's Herndon Command Center and FAA headquarters knew two aircraft had crashed into the World Trade Center. They knew American 77 was lost. At least some FAA officials in Boston Center and the New England Region knew that a hijacker on board American 11 had said "we have some planes." Concerns over the safety of other aircraft began to mount. A manager at the Herndon Command Center asked FAA headquarters if they wanted to order a "nationwide ground stop." While this was being discussed by executives at FAA headquarters, the Command Center ordered one at 9:25.

The Command Center kept looking for American 77. At 9:21, it advised the Dulles terminal control facility, and Dulles urged its controllers to look for primary targets. At 9:32, they found one. Several of the Dulles controllers "observed a primary radar target tracking eastbound at a high rate of speed" and notified Reagan National Airport. FAA personnel at both Reagan National and Dulles airports notified the Secret Service. The aircraft's identity or type was unknown.

At 9:29, the autopilot on American 77 was disengaged; the aircraft was at 7,000 feet and approximately 38 miles west of the Pentagon. At 9:32, controllers at the Dulles Terminal Radar Approach Control "observed a primary radar target tracking eastbound at a high rate of speed." This was later determined to have been Flight 77.

At 9:34, Ronald Reagan Washington National Airport advised the Secret Service of an unknown aircraft heading in the direction of the White House. American 77 was then 5 miles west-southwest of the Pentagon and began a 330-degree turn. At the end of the turn, it was descending through 2,200 feet, pointed toward the Pentagon and downtown Washington. The hijacker pilot then advanced the throttles to maximum power and dove toward the Pentagon.

Barbara Olson, Fox News commentator and wife of the U.S. Solicitor General, was a passenger on Flight 77.

At 9:36, the FAA's Boston Center called NEADS and relayed the discovery about an unidentified aircraft closing in on Washington: "Latest report. Aircraft VFR [visual flight rules] six miles southeast of the White House ... Six, southwest. Six, southwest of the White House, deviating away." This startling news prompted the mission crew commander at NEADS to take immediate control of the airspace to clear a flight path for the Langley fighters: "Okay, we're going to turn it ... crank it up ... Run them to the White House." He then discovered, to his surprise, that the Langley fighters were not headed north toward the Baltimore area as instructed, but east over the ocean. "I don't care how many windows you break," he said. "Damn it ... Okay. Push them back."

After the 9:36 call to NEADS about the unidentified aircraft a few miles from the White House, the Langley fighters were ordered to Washington, D.C. Controllers at NEADS located an unknown primary radar track, but "it kind of faded" over Washington. The time was 9:38. The Pentagon had been struck by American 77 at 9:37:46. The Langley fighters were about 150 miles away.

Right after the Pentagon was hit, NEADS learned of another possible hijacked aircraft. It was an aircraft that in fact had not been hijacked at all. After the second World Trade Center crash, Boston Center managers recognized that both aircraft were transcontinental 767 jetliners that had departed Logan Airport.

Reagan National controllers then vectored an unarmed National Guard C-130H cargo aircraft, which had just taken off en route to Minnesota, to identify and follow the suspicious aircraft. The C-130H pilot spotted it, identified it as a Boeing 757, attempted to follow its path and at 9:38, seconds after impact, reported to the control tower: "looks like that aircraft crashed into the Pentagon sir."

At 9:37:46, American Airlines Flight 77 crashed into the Pentagon, traveling at approximately 530 miles per hour. All on board, as well as many civilian and military personnel in the building, were killed.

The Langley fighters were about 150 miles away

The dome of the Capitol building in Washington, D.C., maintains a silent vigil over the devastation of the Pentagon.

Rescuers challenged flames and deadly smoke to reach those trapped inside the Pentagon (above). The badly injured were evacuated by helicopter (top).

Firefighters and emergency vehicles from hundreds of miles away rushed to the scene to contain the blaze and rescue the injured. The Washington Monument looms in the background as deadly smoke drifts over Washington, D.C.

The symbol of America's military might, the Pentagon, wasn't destroyed by the terrorists. Although extensive damage was done to the west face of the building, there was no disruption of America's military operations.

The Battle for United 93

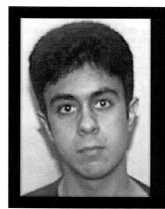   

Department of Justice identifies hijackers: (from left) Alghamdi, Al Haznawi, Alnami, Jarrah

At 8:42, United Airlines Flight 93 took off from Newark (New Jersey) Liberty International Airport bound for San Francisco. The aircraft was piloted by Captain Jason Dahl and First Officer Leroy Homer, and there were five flight attendants. Thirty-seven passengers, including the hijackers, boarded the plane. Scheduled to depart the gate at 8:00, the Boeing 757's takeoff was delayed because of the airport's typically heavy morning traffic.

The hijackers had planned to take flights scheduled to depart at 7:45 (American 11), 8:00 (United 175 and United 93), and 8:10 (American 77). Three of the flights had actually taken off within 10 to 15 minutes of their planned departure times. United 93 would ordinarily have taken off about 15 minutes after pulling away from the gate. When it left the

Beware any cockpit intrusion

ground at 8:42, the flight was running more than 25 minutes late.

As United 93 left Newark, the flight's crew members were unaware of the hijacking of American 11. Around 9:00, the FAA, American, and United were facing the staggering realization of apparent multiple hijackings. At 9:03, they would see another aircraft strike the World Trade Center. Crisis managers at the FAA and the airlines did not yet act to warn other aircraft. At the same time, Boston Center realized that a message transmitted just before 8:25 by the hijacker pilot of American 11 included the phrase, "We have some planes."

FAA controllers at Boston Center, which had tracked the first two hijackings, requested at 9:07 that Herndon Command Center "get messages to airborne aircraft to increase security for the cockpit." There is no evidence that Herndon took such action. Boston Center immediately began speculating about other aircraft that might be in danger, leading them to worry about a transcontinental flight – Delta 1989 – that in fact was not hijacked.

United's first decisive action to notify its airborne aircraft to take defensive action did not come until 9:19, when a United flight dispatcher, Ed Ballinger, took the initiative to begin transmitting warnings to his 16 transcontinental flights: "Beware any cockpit intrusion – Two a/c [aircraft] hit World Trade Center."

One of the flights that received the warning was United 93. Because Ballinger was still responsible for his other flights as well as Flight 175, his warning message was not transmitted to Flight 93 until 9:23.

Jason Dahl, Captain, Flight 93

By all accounts, the first 46 minutes of Flight 93's cross-country trip proceeded routinely. Radio communications from the plane were normal. Heading, speed, and altitude ran according to plan. At 9:24, Ballinger's warning to United 93 was received in the cockpit. Within two minutes, at 9:26, the pilot, Jason Dahl, responded with a note of puzzlement: "Ed, confirm latest mssg plz – Jason."

"Hey get out of here – get out of here – get out of here."

At 9:27, after having been in the air for 45 minutes, United 93 acknowledged a transmission from the Cleveland Center controller. This was the last normal contact the FAA had with the flight.

The Terrorist Strike

The hijackers attacked at 9:28. While traveling 35,000 feet above eastern Ohio, United 93 suddenly dropped 700 feet. Eleven seconds into the descent, the FAA's air traffic control center in Cleveland received the first of two radio transmissions from the aircraft. During the first broadcast, the captain or first officer could be heard declaring "Mayday" amid the sounds of a physical struggle in the cockpit. The second radio transmission, 35 seconds later, indicated that the fight was continuing. The captain or first officer could be heard shouting: "Hey get out of here – get out of here – get out of here."

Less than a minute later, the Cleveland controller and the pilots of aircraft in the vicinity heard "a radio transmission of unintelligible sounds of possible screaming or a struggle from an unknown origin."

The controller responded, seconds later: "Somebody call Cleveland?" This was followed by a second radio transmission, with sounds of screaming. The Cleveland Center controllers began to try to identify the possible source of the transmissions, and noticed that United 93 had descended some 700 feet. The controller attempted again to raise United 93 several times, with no response. At 9:30, the controller began to poll the other flights on his frequency to determine if they had heard the screaming; several said they had.

At 9:32, a hijacker, probably Jarrah, made or attempted to make the following announcement to the passengers of Flight 93:

"Ladies and Gentlemen: Here the captain, please sit down keep remaining sitting. We have a bomb on board. So, sit."

The flight data recorder (also recovered) indicates that Jarrah then instructed the plane's autopilot to turn the aircraft around and head east.

The cockpit voice recorder data indicate that a woman, most likely a flight attendant, was being held captive in the cockpit. She struggled with one of the hijackers who killed or otherwise silenced her.

Passengers Call Their Families

Shortly thereafter, the passengers and flight crew began a series of calls from GTE airphones

Todd Beamer, Cranbury, N.J. He led other passengers in a desperate fight with the hijackers.

Thomas E. Burnett Jr., San Ramon, Calif. He called his wife and told her, "I know we're all going to die - there's three of us who are going to do something about it."

and cellular phones. These calls between family, friends, and colleagues took place until the end of the flight and provided those on the ground with firsthand accounts. They enabled the passengers to gain critical information, including the news that two aircraft had slammed into the World Trade Center.

Between 9:34 and 9:38, the Cleveland controller observed United 93 climbing to 40,700 feet and immediately moved several aircraft out (of) its way. The controller continued to try to contact United 93, and asked whether the pilot could confirm that he had been hijacked. There was no response. Then, at 9:39, a fourth radio transmission was heard from United 93:

Ziad Jarrah: Uh, this is the captain. Would like you all to remain seated. There is a bomb on board and are going back to the airport, and to have our demands [unintelligible]. Please remain quiet.

The controller responded: "United 93, understand you have a bomb on board. Go ahead." The flight did not respond.

While it apparently was not heard by the passengers, this announcement, like those on Flight 11 and Flight 77, was intended to deceive them. Jarrah, like Atta earlier, may have inadvertently broadcast the message because he did not know how to operate the radio and the intercom. To our knowledge none of them had ever flown an actual airliner before.

At least two callers from the flight reported that the hijackers knew that passengers were making calls but did not seem to care. If Jarrah did know that the passengers were making calls, it might not have occurred to him that they were certain to learn what had happened in New York, thereby defeating his attempts at deception.

On Course For Washington, D.C.

At 9:41, Cleveland Center lost United 93's transponder signal. The controller located it on primary radar, matched its position with visual sightings from other aircraft, and tracked the flight as it turned east, then south.

At 9:42, the Command Center learned from news reports that a plane had struck the Pentagon. The Command Center's national operations manager, Ben Sliney, ordered all FAA facilities to instruct all aircraft to land at the nearest airport. This was an unprecedented order. The air traffic control system handled it with great skill, as about 4,500 commercial and general aviation aircraft soon landed without incident.

At 9:46 the Command Center updated FAA

A woman, most likely a flight attendant, was being held captive in the cockpit

headquarters that United 93 was now "twenty-nine minutes out of Washington, D.C."

At 9:49, 13 minutes after Cleveland Center had asked about getting military help, the Command Center suggested that someone at headquarters should decide whether to request military assistance:

FAA Headquarters: They're pulling Jeff away to go talk about United 93.
Command Center: Uh, do we want to think, uh, about scrambling aircraft?
FAA Headquarters: Oh, God, I don't know.
Command Center: Uh, that's a decision somebody's gonna have to make probably in the next ten minutes.
FAA Headquarters: Uh, ya know everybody just left the room.

At least ten passengers and two crew members shared vital information with family, friends, colleagues, or others on the ground. All understood the plane had been hijacked. They said the hijackers wielded knives and claimed to have a bomb. The hijackers were wearing red bandanas, and they forced the passengers to the back of the aircraft.

Callers reported that a passenger had been stabbed and that two people were lying on the floor of the cabin, injured or dead-possibly the captain and first officer. One caller reported that a flight attendant had been killed.

Passengers Make The Ultimate Sacrifice

During at least five of the passengers' phone calls, information was shared about the attacks that had occurred earlier that morning at the World Trade Center. Five calls described the intent of passengers and surviving crew members to revolt against the hijackers. According to one call, they voted on whether to rush the terrorists in an attempt to retake the plane. They decided, and acted.

At 9:57, the passenger assault began. Several passengers had terminated phone calls with loved ones in order to join the revolt. One of the callers ended her message as follows: "Everyone's running up to first class. I've got to go. Bye."

The cockpit voice recorder captured the sounds of the passenger assault muffled by the intervening cockpit door. Some family members who listened to the recording report that they can hear the voice of a loved one among the din. We cannot identify whose voices can be heard. But the assault was sustained.

In response, Jarrah immediately began to roll the airplane to the left and right, attempting to knock the passengers off balance. At 9:58:57, Jarrah told another hijacker in the cockpit to block the door. Jarrah continued to roll the airplane sharply left and right, but the assault continued. At 9:59:52, Jarrah changed tactics and pitched the nose of the airplane up and down to

'Everyone's running up to first class. I've got to go. Bye.'

disrupt the assault. The recorder captured the sounds of loud thumps, crashes, shouts, and breaking glasses and plates. At 10:00:03, Jarrah stabilized the airplane.

Five seconds later, Jarrah asked, "Is that it? Shall we finish it off?" A hijacker responded, "No. Not yet. When they all come, we finish it off." The sounds of fighting continued outside the cockpit. Again, Jarrah pitched the nose of the aircraft up and down.

At 10:00:26, a passenger in the background said, "In the cockpit. If we don't we'll die!" Sixteen seconds later, a passenger yelled, "Roll it!" Jarrah stopped the violent maneuvers at about 10:01:00 and said, "Allah is the greatest! Allah is the greatest!" He then asked another hijacker in the cockpit, "Is that it? I mean, shall we put it down?" to which the other replied, "Yes, put it in it, and pull it down."

(Earlier) at 9:53, FAA headquarters informed the Command Center that the deputy director for air traffic services was talking to Monte Belger about scrambling aircraft. Then the Command Center informed headquarters that controllers had lost track of United 93 over the Pittsburgh area. Within seconds, the Command Center received a visual report from another aircraft, and informed headquarters that the aircraft was 20 miles northwest of Johnstown. United 93 was spotted by another aircraft, and, at 10:01, the Command Center advised FAA headquarters that one of the air-

Passengers on Flight 93 (from left): Alan Beaven, Hurleyville, N.Y.; Deora Frances Bodley, San Diego, Calif.; Joseph Deluca, Ledgewood, N.J.; Sandra W. Bradshaw, Greensboro, N.C.

craft had seen United 93 "waving his wings." The aircraft had witnessed the hijackers' efforts to defeat the passengers' counterattack.

The passengers continued their assault and at 10:02:23, a hijacker said, "Pull it down! Pull it down!" The hijackers remained at the controls but must have judged that the passengers were only seconds from overcoming them. The airplane headed down; the control wheel was turned hard to the right. The airplane rolled onto its back, and one of the hijackers began shouting "Allah is the greatest. Allah is the greatest." With the sounds of the passenger counterattack continuing, the aircraft

This artist rendering, part of a tribute to the heroes of Flight 93, depicts how the passengers may have attacked the hijackers.

plowed into an empty field in Shanksville, Pennsylvania, at 580 miles per hour, about 20 minutes flying time from Washington, D.C.

Despite the discussions about military assistance, no one from FAA headquarters requested military assistance regarding United 93. Nor did any manager at FAA headquarters pass any of the information it had about United 93 to the military.

Jarrah's objective was to crash his airliner into symbols of the American Republic, the Capitol or the White House. He was defeated by the alerted, unarmed passengers of United 93.

Smoke fills the woods behind the debris field where Flight 93 crashed near Shanksville, Pa. Investigators combed the area looking for clues.

Only days after the crash, residents of this small Pennsylvania town held a memorial service at the site to honor the heroes of Flight 93.

The Hijacking of United 175

Department of Justice identifies hijackers: Al-Shehhi, Ahmed Alghamdi, Banihammad, Hamza Alghamdi, Alshehri.

United Airlines Flight 175 was scheduled to depart for Los Angeles at 8:00. Captain Victor Saracini and First Officer Michael Horrocks piloted the Boeing 767, which had seven flight attendants. Fifty-six passengers boarded the flight.

The flight had taken off just as American 11 was being hijacked, and at 8:42 the United 175 flight crew completed their report on a "suspicious transmission" overheard from another plane (which turned out to have been Flight 11) just after takeoff.

An Ominous Warning

Shortly after entering New York Center's airspace, the pilot of United 175 broke in with the following transmission:

UAL 175: New York UAL 175 heavy.

FAA: UAL 175 go ahead.

UAL 175: Yeah. We figured we'd wait to go to your center. Ah, we heard a suspicious transmission on our departure out of Boston, ah, with someone, ah, it sounded like someone keyed the mikes and said ah everyone ah stay in your seats.

FAA: Oh, okay. I'll pass that along over here.

'It's getting bad, Dad'

This was United 175's last communication with the ground. The hijackers attacked sometime between 8:42 and 8:46. They used knives (as reported by two passengers and a flight attendant), Mace (reported by one passenger), and the threat of a bomb (reported by the same passenger). They stabbed members of the flight crew (reported by a flight attendant and one passenger). Both pilots had been killed (reported by one flight attendant).

Minutes later, United 175 turned southwest without clearance from air traffic control. At 8:47, seconds after the impact of American 11, United 175's transponder code changed, and then changed again. These changes were not noticed for several minutes, however, because the same New York Center controller was assigned to both American 11 and United 175. The controller knew American 11 was hijacked; he was focused on searching for it after the aircraft disappeared at 8:46.

The first operational evidence that something was abnormal on United 175 came at 8:47, when the aircraft changed beacon codes twice within a minute. At 8:51, the flight deviated from its assigned altitude, and a minute later New York air traffic controllers began repeatedly and unsuccessfully trying to contact it.

At 8:48, while the controller was still trying to locate American 11, a New York Center manager provided the following report on a Command Center teleconference about American 11:

Manager, New York Center: Okay. This is New York Center. We're watching the airplane. I also had conversation with American Airlines, and they've told us that they believe that one of their stewardesses was stabbed and that there are people in the cockpit that have control of the air-craft, and that's all the information they have right now.

Beginning at 8:52, the controller made repeated attempts to reach the crew of United 175. Still no response. The controller checked his radio equipment and contacted another controller at 8:53, saying that "we may have a hijack" and that he could not find the aircraft.

A Son Calls His Father

At 8:52, in Easton, Connecticut, a man named Lee Hanson received a phone call from his son Peter, a passenger on United 175. His son told him: "I think they've taken over the cockpit – An attendant has been stabbed – and someone else up front may have been killed. The plane is making strange moves. Call United Airlines – Tell them it's Flight 175, Boston to LA." Lee Hanson then called the Easton Police Department and relayed what he had heard.

At about 8:55, the controller in charge notified a New York Center manager that she believed United 175 had also been hijacked. The manager tried to notify the regional managers and was told that they were discussing a hijacked aircraft (presumably American 11) and refused to be disturbed. At 8:58, the New York Center controller searching for United 175 told another New York controller "we might have a hijack over here, two of them."

At 8:58, the flight took a heading toward New

Garnet Ace Bailey, passenger

York City. At 8:59, Flight 175 passenger Brian David Sweeney tried to call his wife, Julie. He left a message on their home answering machine that the plane had been hijacked. He then called his mother, Louise Sweeney, told her the flight had been hijacked, and added that the passengers were thinking about storming the cockpit to take control of the plane away from the hijackers.

Between 9:01 and 9:02, a manager from New York Center told the Command Center in Herndon:

Manager, New York Center: We have several situations going on here. It's escalating big, big time. We need to get the military involved with us. ... We're, we're involved with something else, we have other aircraft that may have a similar situation going on here.

The "other aircraft" referred to by New York Center was United 175. Evidence indicates that this conversation was the only notice received by either FAA headquarters or the Herndon Command Center prior to the second crash that there had been a second hijacking.

While the Command Center was told about this "other aircraft" at 9:01, New York Center contacted New York terminal approach control and asked for help in locating United.

Terminal: I got somebody who keeps coasting but it looks like he's going into one of the small airports down there.

Al Marchand, a retired Alamogordo Department of Public Safety lieutenant, was a flight attendant on United 175.

Center: Hold on a second. I'm trying to bring him up here and get you – There he is right there. Hold on.

Terminal: Got him just out of 9,500-9,000 now.

Center: Do you know who he is?

Terminal: We're just, we just we don't know who he is. We're just picking him up now.

Center (at 9:02): Alright. Heads up man, it looks like another one coming in.

Father Listens To Son's Last Moment ...

At 9:00, Lee Hanson received a second call from his son Peter: "It's getting bad, Dad – A stewardess was stabbed – They seem to have knives and Mace – They said they have a bomb – It's getting very bad on the plane – Passengers are throwing up and getting sick – The plane is making jerky movements – I don't think the pilot is flying the plane – I think we are going down – I think they intend to go to Chicago or someplace and fly into a building – Don't worry, Dad – If it happens, it'll be very fast – My God, my God."

The call ended abruptly. Lee Hanson had heard a woman scream just before it cut off. He turned on a television, and in her home so did Louise Sweeney. Both then saw the second aircraft hit the World Trade Center.

At 9:03:11, United Airlines Flight 175 struck the South Tower of the World Trade Center. All on board, along with an unknown number of people in the tower, were killed instantly.

Within minutes of the second impact, Boston Center instructed its controllers to inform all aircraft in its airspace of the events in New York and to advise aircraft to heighten cockpit security. Boston Center asked the

It looks like another one coming in

Herndon Command Center to issue a similar cockpit security alert nationwide. We have found no evidence to suggest that the Command Center acted on this request or issued any type of cockpit security alert.

This incredible photo shows Flight 175 on a deadly path to the South Tower. The North Tower, struck 17 minutes earlier, is burning furiously.

A Nation Transformed

More than 2,600 people died at the World Trade Center; 125 died at the Pentagon; 256 died on the four planes. The death toll surpassed that at Pearl Harbor in December 1941.

This immeasurable pain was inflicted by 19 young Arabs acting at the behest of Islamist extremists headquartered in distant Afghanistan. Some had been in the United States for more than a year, mixing with the rest of the population. Though four had training as pilots, most were not well-educated. Most spoke English poorly, some hardly at all.

Why did they do this? How was the attack planned and conceived? How did the U.S. government fail to anticipate and prevent it? What can we do in the future to prevent similar acts of terrorism?

A Shock, Not A Surprise

The 9/11 attacks were a shock, but they should not have come as a surprise. Islamist extremists had given plenty of warning that they meant to kill Americans indiscriminately and in large numbers.

A History Of Terror

In February 1993, a group led by Ramzi Yousef tried to bring down the World Trade Center with a truck bomb. They killed six and wounded a thousand. Plans by Omar Abdel Rahman and others to blow up the Holland and Lincoln tunnels and other New York City landmarks were frustrated when the plotters were arrested.

In early 1995, police in Manila uncovered a plot by Ramzi Yousef to blow up a dozen U.S. airliners while they were flying over the Pacific. In November 1995, a car bomb exploded outside the office of the U.S. program manager for the Saudi National Guard in Riyadh, killing five Americans and two others. In June 1996, a truck bomb demolished the Khobar Towers apartment complex in Dhahran, Saudi Arabia, killing 19 U.S. servicemen and wounding hundreds. The attack was carried out primarily by Saudi Hezbollah, an organization that had received help from the government of Iran.

Until 1997, the U.S. intelligence community viewed Bin Ladin as a financier of terrorism, not as a terrorist leader. In February 1998, Usama Bin Ladin and four others issued a self-styled fatwa, publicly declaring that it was God's decree that every Muslim should try his utmost to kill any American, military or civilian, anywhere in the world, because of American "occupation" of Islam's holy places and aggression against Muslims.

> *Usama Bin Ladin: Every Muslim should try his utmost to kill any American*

President Bush, at a school in Florida, the moment he received the news of the attacks on the World Trade Center.

In August 1998, Bin Ladin's group, al Qaeda, carried out near-simultaneous truck bomb attacks on the U.S. embassies in Nairobi, Kenya, and Dar es Salaam, Tanzania. The attacks killed 224 people, including 12 Americans, and wounded thousands more.

Debate about what to do settled very soon on one option: Tomahawk cruise missiles. General Hugh Shelton, the chairman of the Joint Chiefs of Staff, had directed General Zinni at Central Command to develop a plan, which he had submitted during the first week of July. Zinni's planners surely considered the two previous times the United States had used force to respond to terrorism, the 1986 strike on Libya and the 1993 strike against Iraq. They proposed firing Tomahawks against eight terrorist camps

 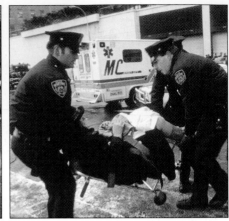 

The terrorists who bombed the World Trade Center in 1993, Ismoil (left) and Yousef were found guilty. Rescue workers (center) treat a victim of the first WTC attack. (Right) In 1996, terrorists exploded a truck bomb at a U.S. military facility in Saudi Arabia.

in Afghanistan, including Bin Ladin's compound at Tarnak Farms.

Considerable debate went to the question of whether to strike targets outside of Afghanistan, including two facilities in Sudan. One was a tannery believed to belong to Bin Ladin. The other was al Shifa, a Khartoum pharmaceutical plant, which intelligence reports said was manufacturing a precursor ingredient for nerve gas with Bin Ladin's financial support. The argument for hitting the tannery was that it could hurt Bin Ladin financially. The argument for hitting al Shifa was that it would lessen the chance of Bin Ladin's having nerve gas for a later attack.

On August 20, Navy vessels in the Arabian Sea fired their cruise missiles. Though most of

'When these attacks occur, as they likely will, we will wonder what more we could have done to stop them'

them hit their intended targets, neither Bin Ladin nor any other terrorist leader was killed. Berger told us that an after-action review by Director Tenet concluded that the strikes had killed 20-30 people in the camps but probably missed Bin Ladin by a few hours.

In December 1999, Jordanian police foiled a plot to bomb hotels and other sites frequented by American tourists, and a U.S. Customs agent arrested Ahmed Ressam at the U.S. Canadian border as he was smuggling in explosives intended for an attack on Los Angeles International Airport.

In October 2000, an al Qaeda team in Aden, Yemen, used a motorboat filled with explosives to blow a hole in the side of a destroyer, the *USS Cole*, almost sinking the vessel and killing 17 American sailors. The 9/11 attacks on the World Trade Center and the

Ahmed Ghailani (left) was suspected of bombing the U.S. Embassy (center and right) in Nairobi in 1998.

Pentagon were far more elaborate, precise, and destructive than any of these earlier assaults. But by September 2001, the executive branch of the U.S. government, the Congress, the news media, and the American public had received clear warning that Islamist terrorists meant to kill Americans in high numbers.

Usama Steps Forward

In the 1980s, young Muslims from around the world went to Afghanistan to join as volunteers in a jihad (or holy struggle) against the Soviet Union. A wealthy Saudi, Usama Bin Ladin, was one of them. Following the defeat of the Soviets in the late 1980s, Bin Ladin and others formed al Qaeda to mobilize jihads elsewhere.

The history, culture, and body of beliefs from which Bin Ladin shapes and spreads his message are largely unknown to many Americans.

Seizing on symbols of Islam's past greatness, he promises to restore pride to people who consider themselves the victims of successive foreign masters. He uses cultural and religious allusions to the holy Qur'an and some of its interpreters. Bin Ladin also stresses grievances against the United States widely shared in the Muslim world.

The *USS Cole* (above) was attacked by Al-Badawi (above right) and Al-Qusu (above left). Seventeen American sailors were killed in the 2000 attack.

 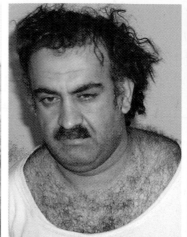 

Usama Bin Ladin as a young fighter in Afghanistan (left). Terrorist Khalid Shaikh Mohammed was captured in 2003 (center). The only terrorist convicted so far for the 9/11 attacks is Mounir El Motassadeq (right).

1998 To September 11, 2001 – The 'Planes Operation'

The August 1998 bombings of U.S. embassies in Kenya and Tanzania established al Qaeda as a potent adversary of the United States.

After launching cruise missile strikes against al Qaeda targets in Afghanistan and Sudan in retaliation for the embassy bombings, the Clinton administration applied diplomatic pressure to try to persuade the Taliban regime in Afghanistan to expel Bin Ladin. The administration also devised covert operations to use CIA-paid foreign agents to capture or kill Bin Ladin and his chief lieutenants. These actions did not stop Bin Ladin or dislodge al Qaeda from its sanctuary.

By late 1998 or early 1999, Bin Ladin and his advisers had agreed on an idea brought to them by

The al Qaeda operatives lived openly in San Diego under their true names

Khalid Sheikh Mohammed (KSM) called the "planes operation." It would eventually culminate in the 9/ 11 attacks.

KSM claims that his original plot was even grander than those carried out on 9/11 – ten planes would attack targets on both the East and West coasts of the United States. Bin Ladin provided KSM with four initial operatives for suicide plane attacks within the United States, and in the fall of 1999 training for the attacks began. New recruits included four from a cell of expatriate Muslim extremists who had clustered together in Hamburg, Germany. One became the tactical commander of the operation in the United States: Mohamed Atta. U.S. intelligence frequently picked up reports of attacks planned by al Qaeda.

Terrorists Arrive In America

In January 2000, the intense intelligence

effort glimpsed and then lost sight of two operatives destined for the "planes operation." Spotted in Kuala Lumpur, the pair were lost passing through Bangkok. On January 15, 2000, they arrived in Los Angeles.

We do know that soon after arriving in California, the two al Qaeda operatives sought out and found a group of ideologically like-minded Muslims with roots in Yemen and Saudi Arabia, individuals mainly associated with a young Yemeni and others who attended a mosque in San Diego. After a brief stay in Los Angeles about which we know little, the al Qaeda operatives lived openly in San Diego under their true names. They managed to avoid attracting much attention.

By the summer of 2000, three of the four Hamburg cell members had arrived on the East Coast of the United States and had begun pilot training. In early 2001, a fourth future hijacker pilot, Hani Hanjour, journeyed to Arizona with another operative, Nawaf al Hazmi, and conducted his refresher pilot training there. A number of al Qaeda operatives had spent time in Arizona during the 1980s and early 1990s.

Waiting For Intelligence Reports

During 2000, President Bill Clinton and his advisers renewed diplomatic efforts to get Bin Ladin expelled from Afghanistan. They also

The President and the National Security Team meet to discuss military action taken against Afghanistan.

renewed secret efforts with some of the Taliban's opponents – the Northern Alliance – to get enough intelligence to attack Bin Ladin directly. Diplomatic efforts centered on the new military government in Pakistan, and they did not succeed. The efforts with the Northern Alliance revived an inconclusive and secret debate about whether the United States should take sides in Afghanistan's civil war and support the Taliban's enemies. The CIA also produced a plan to improve intelligence collection on al Qaeda, including the use of a small, unmanned airplane with a video camera, known as the Predator.

After the October 2000 attack on the *USS Cole*, evidence accumulated that it had been launched by al Qaeda operatives, but without confirmation that Bin Ladin had given the order. The Taliban had earlier been warned that it would be held responsible for another Bin Ladin attack on the United States. The CIA described its findings as a "preliminary judgment"; President Clinton and his chief advisers told us they were waiting for a conclusion before deciding whether to take military action. The military alternatives remained unappealing to them.

As part of the response to the embassy

A member of al Qaeda at a secret training camp near Kabul, 2001.

Usama Bin Ladin, was the mastermind behind the 9/11 attacks.

bombings, President Clinton signed a Memorandum of Notification authorizing the CIA to let its tribal assets use force to capture Bin Ladin and his associates. CIA officers told the tribals that the plan to capture Bin Ladin, which had been "turned off" three months earlier, was back on. The memorandum also authorized the CIA to attack Bin Ladin in other ways. Also, an executive order froze financial holdings that could be linked to Bin Ladin.

The counterterrorism staff at CIA thought it was gaining a better understanding of Bin Ladin and his network. In preparation for briefing the Senate Select Committee on Intelligence on September 2, Tenet was told that the intelligence community knew more about Bin Ladin's network "than about any other top tier terrorist organization."

CIA Briefs The Presidents

In early September 2000, Acting Deputy Director of Central Intelligence John McLaughlin led a team to Bush's ranch in Crawford, Texas, and gave him a wide-ranging, four-hour review of sensitive information. Ben Bonk, deputy chief of the CIA's Counterterrorist Center, used one of the four hours to deal with terrorism. To highlight the danger of terrorists obtaining chemical, biological, radiological, or nuclear weapons, Bonk brought along a mock-up suitcase to evoke the way the Aum Shinrikyo doomsday cult had spread deadly sarin nerve agent on the Tokyo subway in 1995. Bonk told Bush that Americans would die from terrorism during the next four years.

In December, Bush met with Clinton for a two-hour, one-on-one discussion of national security and foreign policy challenges. Clinton recalled saying to Bush, "I think you will find that by far your biggest threat is Bin Ladin and the al Qaeda." Clinton told us that he also said, "One of the great regrets of my presidency is

President Bush is congratulated by President Clinton at his inauguration in 2001.
Bush expanded the war against terror. ?

From Left: Attorney General John Ashcroft, Sheikh Omar Abdel-Rahman convicted of terrorist conspiracy, and CIA Director George Tenet

that I didn't get him [Bin Ladin] for you, because I tried to."

The transition to the new Bush administration in late 2000 and early 2001 took place with the Cole issue still pending. President George W. Bush and his chief advisers accepted that al Qaeda was responsible for the attack on the *Cole*, but did not like the options available for a response.

Warnings

During the spring and summer of 2001, U.S. intelligence agencies received a stream of warnings that al Qaeda planned, as one report put it, "something very, very, very big." Director of Central Intelligence George Tenet told us, "The system was blinking red."

During 2001, Director of Central Intelligence George Tenet was briefed regularly regarding threats and other operational information relating to Usama Bin Ladin. He in turn met daily with President Bush, who was briefed by the CIA through what is known as the President's Daily Brief (PDB). There were more than 40 intelligence articles in the PDBs from January 20 to September 10, 2001, that related to Bin Ladin.

In the spring of 2001, the level of reporting on terrorist threats and planned attacks increased dramatically to its highest level since the millennium alert. On March 23, in connection with discussions about possibly reopening Pennsylvania Avenue in front of the White House, Richard C. Clarke warned National Security Advisor Condoleezza Rice that domestic or foreign terrorists might use a truck bomb – their "weapon of choice" – on Pennsylvania Avenue. That would result, he said, in the destruction of the West Wing and parts of the residence. He also told her that he thought there were terrorist cells within the United States, including al Qaeda.

In May 2001, the drumbeat of reporting grew

louder with reports to top officials that "Bin Ladin public profile may presage attack" and "Bin Ladin network's plans advancing." In early May, a walk-in to the FBI claimed there was a plan to launch attacks on London, Boston, and New York. Attorney General John Ashcroft was briefed by the CIA on May 15 regarding al Qaeda generally and the current threat reporting specifically. The next day brought a report that a phone call to a U.S. embassy had warned that Bin Ladin supporters were planning an attack in the United States using "high explosives."

On May 17, based on the previous day's report, the first item on the CSG's agenda was "UBL: Operation Planned in U.S." The anonymous caller's tip could not be corroborated. Late May brought reports of a possible hostage plot against Americans abroad to force the release of prisoners, including Sheikh Omar Abdel Rahman, the "Blind Sheikh," who was serving a life sentence for his role in the 1993 plot to blow up sites in New York City. The reporting noted that operatives might opt to hijack an aircraft or storm a U.S. embassy. This report led to a Federal Aviation Administration (FAA) information circular to airlines noting the potential for "an airline hijacking to free terrorists incarcerated in the United States."

Other reporting mentioned that Abu Zubaydah was planning an attack, possibly against Israel, and expected to carry out several

Former White House counterterrorism chief Richard A. Clarke

more if things went well. On May 24 alone, counterterrorism officials grappled with reports alleging plots in Yemen and Italy, as well as a report about a cell in Canada that an anonymous caller had claimed might be planning an attack against the United States.

Reports similar to many of these were made available to President Bush in morning intelligence briefings with DCI Tenet, usually attended by Vice President Dick Cheney and National Security Advisor Rice. While these briefings discussed general threats to attack America and American interests, the specific threats mentioned in these briefings were all overseas. On May 29, Clarke suggested that Rice ask DCI Tenet what more the United States could do to stop Abu Zubaydah from launching "a series of major terrorist attacks," probably on Israeli targets, but possibly on U.S. facilities.

Clarke wrote to Rice and her deputy, Stephen Hadley, "When these attacks occur, as they likely will, we will wonder what more we could have done to stop them." In May, CIA Counterterrorist Center (CTC) Chief Cofer Black told Rice that the current threat level was a 7 on a scale of 1 to 10, as compared to an 8 during the millennium.

A terrorist threat advisory distributed in late June indicated a high probability of near-term "spectacular" terrorist attacks resulting in numerous casualties. Other reports' titles warned, "Bin Ladin Attacks May be Imminent" and "Bin Ladin and Associates Making Near-Term Threats." The latter reported multiple attacks planned over the coming days, including a "severe blow" against U.S. and Israeli "interests" during the next two weeks.

On June 25, Clarke warned Rice and Hadley that six separate intelligence reports showed al Qaeda personnel warning of a pending attack. An Arabic television station reported Bin Ladin's pleasure with al Qaeda leaders who were saying that the next weeks "will witness important surprises" and that U.S. and Israeli interests will be targeted. Al Qaeda also released a new recruitment and fund-raising tape. Clarke wrote that this was all too sophisticated to be merely a psychological operation to keep the United States on edge, and the CIA agreed. The intelligence reporting consistently described the upcoming attacks as occurring on a calamitous level, indicating that they would cause the world to be in turmoil and that they would consist of possible multiple – but not necessarily simultaneous – attacks.

On June 28, Clarke wrote Rice that the pattern of al Qaeda activity indicating attack planning over the past six weeks "had reached a crescendo." One al Qaeda intelligence report warned that something "very, very, very, very" big was about to happen, and most of Bin

Dr. Condoleezza Rice, National Security Advisor

Ladin's network was reportedly anticipating the attack.

The headline of a June 30 briefing to top officials was stark: "Bin Ladin Planning High-Profile Attacks." The report stated that Bin Ladin operatives expected near-term attacks to have dramatic consequences of catastrophic proportions.

Although Bin Ladin was determined to strike in the United States, as President Clinton had been told and President Bush was reminded in a Presidential Daily Brief article briefed to him in August 2001, the specific threat information pointed overseas.

The threat did not receive national media attention comparable to the millennium alert. Though the "planes operation" was progressing, the plotters had problems of their own in 2001. Several possible participants dropped out; others could not gain entry into the United States. Zacarias Moussaoui, who showed up at a flight training school in Minnesota, may have been a candidate to replace him.

On August 15, 2001, the Minneapolis FBI Field Office initiated an intelligence investigation on Zacarias Moussaoui. Moussaoui stood out because, with little knowledge of flying, he wanted to learn how to "take off and land" a Boeing 747. The agent in Minneapolis quickly learned that Moussaoui possessed jihadist beliefs. Moreover, Moussaoui had $32,000 in a bank account but did not provide a plausible explanation for this sum of money. He had traveled to Pakistan but became agitated when asked if he had traveled to nearby countries while in Pakistan (Pakistan was the customary route to the training camps in Afghanistan).

Some of the vulnerabilities of the plotters become clear in retrospect. Moussaoui aroused suspicion for seeking fast-track

Zacarias Moussaoui charged with conspiracy in the 9/11 attacks.

training on how to pilot large jet airliners. He was arrested on August 16, 2001, for violations of immigration regulations. In late August, officials in the intelligence community realized that the terrorists spotted in Southeast Asia in January 2000 had arrived in the United States.

These cases did not prompt urgent action. In the words of one official, no analytic work foresaw the lightning that could connect the thundercloud to the ground.

Hijacker Mohamed Atta attended this flight school in Lantana, Fla.

Why The System Failed To Protect America

The most important failure was one of imagination. We do not believe leaders understood the gravity of the threat. As late as September 4, 2001, Richard Clarke, the White House staffer long responsible for counterterrorism policy coordination, asserted that the government had not yet made up its mind how to answer the question: "Is al Qaeda a big deal?"

A week later came the answer.

The CIA

Before 9/11, the United States tried to solve the al Qaeda problem with the capabilities it had used in the last stages of the Cold War and its immediate aftermath. These capabilities were insufficient. Little was done to expand or reform them. The CIA had minimal capacity to conduct paramilitary operations with its own personnel, and it did not seek a large-scale expansion of these capabilities before 9/11.

The Department Of Defense

At no point before 9/11 was the Department of Defense fully engaged in the mission of countering al Qaeda, even though this was perhaps the most dangerous foreign enemy threatening the United States. America's homeland defenders faced outward. NORAD itself was barely able to retain any alert bases at all. Its planning scenarios occasionally considered the danger of hijacked aircraft being guided to American targets, but only aircraft that were coming from overseas.

The FBI

The most serious weaknesses in agency capabilities were in the domestic arena. The FBI did not have the capability to link the collective knowledge of agents in the field to national priorities. Other domestic agencies deferred to the FBI.

The FAA

FAA capabilities were weak. Any serious examination of the possibility of a suicide hijacking could have suggested changes to fix glaring vulnerabilities – expanding no-fly lists, searching passengers identified by the CAPPS screening system, deploying federal air marshals domestically, hardening cockpit doors, alerting air crews to a different kind of hijacking possibility than they had been trained to expect. Yet the FAA did not adjust either its own training or training with NORAD to take account of threats other than those experienced in the past.

America stood out as an object for admiration, envy, and blame. This created a kind of cultural asymmetry. To us, Afghanistan seemed very far away. To members of al Qaeda, America seemed very close. In a sense, they were more globalized than we were.

If the government's leaders understood the gravity of the threat they faced and understood at the same time that their policies to eliminate it were not likely to succeed any time soon, then history's judgment will be harsh. Did they understand the gravity of the threat?

The U.S. Embassy in Nairobi after a terrorist bombing attack.

The *USS Cole* after a terrorist bomb killed 17 American sailors.

Assessing The Threat

Before 9/11, al Qaeda and its affiliates had killed fewer than 50 Americans, including the East Africa embassy bombings and the *Cole* attack. The U.S. government took the threat seriously, but not in the sense of mustering anything like the kind of effort that would be gathered to confront an enemy of the first, second, or even third rank. The modest national effort exerted to contain Serbia and its depredations in the Balkans between 1995 and 1999, for example, was orders of magnitude larger than that devoted to al Qaeda.

By 2001 the government still needed a decision at the highest level as to whether al Qaeda was or was not "a first order threat," Richard Clarke wrote in his first memo to Condoleezza Rice on January 25, 2001. In his blistering protest about foot-dragging in the Pentagon and at the CIA, sent to Rice just a week before 9/11, he repeated that the "real question" for the principals was "are we serious about dealing with the al Qaeda threat? ... Is al Qaeda a big deal?" One school of thought, Clarke wrote in this September 4 note, implicitly argued that the terrorist network was a nuisance that killed a score of Americans every 18-24 months. If that

From Left: Richard Clarke, former White House counterterror chief; Condoleezza Rice, National Security Advisor; Vice President Gore gives President Clinton a report on Aviation Safety and Security in 1997; a piece of the wing of TWA Flight 800 floats in the waters off Long Island, 1996.

view was credited, then current policies might be proportionate. Another school saw al Qaeda as the "point of the spear of radical Islam."

A Warning In 1998

In 1996, as a result of the TWA Flight 800 crash, President Clinton created a commission under Vice President Al Gore to report on shortcomings in aviation security in the United States. The Gore Commission's report, having thoroughly canvassed available expertise in and outside of government, did not mention suicide hijackings or the use of aircraft as weapons. It focused mainly on the danger of placing bombs onto aircraft-the approach of the Manila air plot. The Gore Commission did call attention, however, to lax screening of passengers and what they carried onto planes. In late 1998, reports came in of a possible al Qaeda plan to hijack a plane.

Threat reports also mentioned the possibility of using an aircraft filled with explosives. The

The 9/11 hijackers included known al Qaeda operatives who could have been watch-listed

most prominent of these mentioned a possible plot to fly an explosives-laden aircraft into a U.S. city. This report, circulated in September 1998, originated from a source who had walked into an American consulate in East Asia.

One prescient pre-9/11 analysis of an aircraft plot was written by a Justice Department trial attorney. The attorney had taken an interest, apparently on his own initiative, in the legal issues that would be involved in shooting down a U.S. aircraft in such a situation.

NORAD

The North American Aerospace Defense Command imagined the possible use of aircraft as weapons, too, and developed exercises to counter such a threat-from planes coming to the United States from overseas, perhaps carrying a weapon of mass destruction. None of this speculation was based on actual intelligence of

The movie _Pearl Harbor_ recreated the explosion of the _USS SHAW_ on December 7, 1941, during the Japanese attack.

such a threat. One idea, intended to test command and control plans and NORAD's readiness, postulated a hijacked airliner coming from overseas and crashing into the Pentagon. The idea was put aside in the early planning of the exercise as too much of a distraction from the main focus (war in Korea), and as too unrealistic. As we pointed out in chapter 1, the military planners assumed that since such aircraft would be coming from overseas; they would have time to identify the target and scramble interceptors.

We can therefore establish that at least some government agencies were concerned about the hijacking danger and had speculated about various scenarios. The challenge was to flesh out

and test those scenarios, then figure out a way to turn a scenario into constructive action.

Failure To Protect Against Surprise Attacks

Since the Pearl Harbor attack of 1941, the intelligence community has devoted generations of effort to understanding the problem of forestalling a surprise attack. Rigorous analytic methods were developed, focused in particular on the Soviet Union, and several leading practitioners within the intelligence community discussed them with us. These methods have been articulated in many ways, but almost all seem to have at least four elements in common: (1) think about how surprise attacks might be launched; (2) identify telltale indicators connected to the most dangerous possibilities; (3) where feasible, collect intelligence on these indicators; and (4) adopt defenses to deflect the most dangerous possibilities or at least trigger an earlier warning. After the end of the Gulf War, concerns about lack of warning led to a major study conducted for DCI Robert Gates in 1992 that proposed several recommendations, among them strengthening the national intelligence officer for warning. We were told that these measures languished under Gates' successors. Responsibility for warning related to a terrorist attack passed from the national intelligence officer for warning to the CTC. An Intelligence Community Counterterrorism Board had the responsibility to issue threat advisories.

CIA Director Robert Gates, 1992

Zacarias Moussaoui, the only person charged in the 9/11 attacks.

With the important exception of analysis of al Qaeda efforts in chemical, biological, radiological, and nuclear weapons, we did not find evidence that the methods to avoid surprise attack that had been so laboriously developed over the years were regularly applied. Considering what was not done suggests possible ways to institutionalize imagination.

To return to the four elements of analysis just mentioned:

1. The CTC did not analyze how an aircraft, hijacked or explosives-laden, might be used as a weapon. It did not perform this kind of analysis from the enemy's perspective ("red team" analysis), even though suicide terrorism had become a principal tactic of Middle Eastern terrorists. If it had done so, we believe such an analysis would soon have spotlighted a critical constraint for the terrorists-finding a suicide operative able to fly large jet aircraft. They had never done so before 9/11.

2. The CTC did not develop a set of telltale indicators for this method of attack. For example, one such indicator might be the discovery of possible terrorists pursuing flight training to fly large jet aircraft, or seeking to buy advanced flight simulators.

3. The CTC did not propose, and the intelligence community collection management process did not set, requirements to monitor such telltale indicators. Therefore the warning system was not looking for information such as the July 2001 FBI report of potential terrorist interest in various kinds of aircraft training in Arizona, or the August 2001 arrest of Zacarias Moussaoui because of his suspicious behavior in a Minnesota flight school. In late August, the Moussaoui arrest was briefed to the DCI and other top CIA officials under the head-

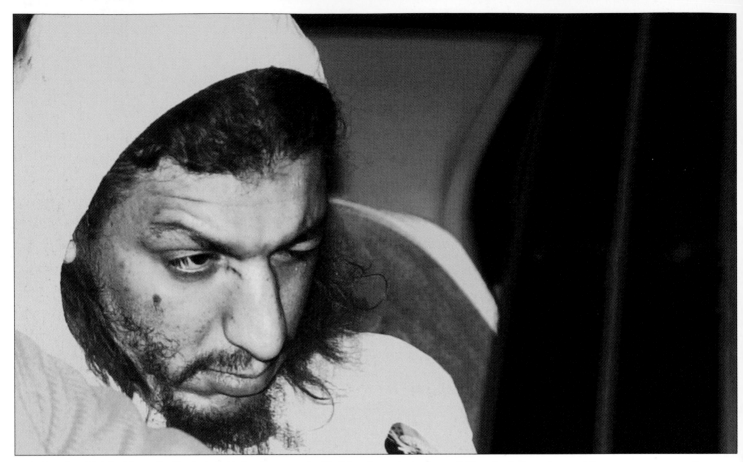

Richard Reid tried to set off a bomb he had concealed in his shoe aboard an airliner but was stopped by passengers and crew.

ing "Islamic Extremist Learns to Fly." Because the system was not tuned to comprehend the potential significance of this information, the news had no effect on warning.

4. Neither the intelligence community nor aviation security experts analyzed systemic defenses within an aircraft or against terrorist controlled aircraft, suicidal or otherwise. The many threat reports mentioning aircraft were passed to the FAA. While that agency continued to react to specific, credible threats, it did not try to perform the broader warning functions we describe here. No one in the government was taking on that role for domestic vulnerabilities. Richard Clarke told us that he was concerned about the danger posed by aircraft in the context of protecting the Atlanta Olympics of 1996, the White House complex, and the 2001 G-8 summit in Genoa. But he attributed his awareness more to Tom Clancy novels than to warnings from the intelligence community. He did not, or could not, press the government to work on the systemic issues of how to strengthen the layered security defenses to protect aircraft against hijackings or put the adequacy of air defenses against suicide hijackers on the national policy agenda. The methods for detecting and then warning of surprise attack that the U.S. government had so painstakingly developed in the decades after Pearl Harbor did not fail; instead, they were not really tried. They were not employed to analyze the enemy that, as

The President is briefed on the military activity in Iraq by VP Cheney (foreground, left), CIA Director George Tenet (left) and Andy Card, Chief of Staff.

the twentieth century closed, was most likely to launch a surprise attack directly against the United States.

Underestimating The Enemy

The road to 9/11 again illustrates how the large, unwieldy U.S. government tended to underestimate a threat that grew ever greater. The terrorism fostered by Bin Ladin and al Qaeda was different from anything the government had faced before. The existing mechanisms for handling terrorist acts had been trial and punishment for acts committed by individuals; sanction, reprisal, deterrence, or war for acts by hostile governments. The actions of al Qaeda fit neither catego-

ry. Its crimes were on a scale approaching acts of war, but they were committed by a loose, far-flung, nebulous conspiracy with no territories or citizens or assets that could be readily threatened, overwhelmed, or destroyed.

In response to the request of policymakers, the military prepared an array of limited strike options for attacking Bin Ladin and his organization from May 1998 onward.

On three specific occasions in 1998 and 1999, intelligence was deemed credible enough to warrant planning for possible strikes to kill Bin Ladin. But in each case the strikes did not go forward, because senior policymakers did not regard the intelligence as sufficiently actionable to offset their assessment of the risks.

The Director of Central Intelligence, policy-makers, and military officials expressed frustration with the lack of actionable intelligence. Some officials inside the Pentagon, including those in the special forces and the counterterrorism policy office, also expressed frustration with the lack of military action.

Government Agencies Failed To Institute Changes

Before 9/11, no agency did more to attack al Qaeda than the CIA. But there were limits to what the CIA was able to achieve by disrupting terrorist activities abroad and by using proxies to try to capture Bin Ladin and his lieutenants in Afghanistan.

Throughout the 1990s, the FBI's counterterrorism efforts against international terrorist organizations included both intelligence and criminal investigations. The FBI's approach to investigations was case-specific, decentralized, and geared toward prosecution. Significant FBI resources were devoted to after-the-fact investigations of major terrorist attacks, resulting in several prosecutions.

The FBI attempted several reform efforts

The White House is high on the list of targets for terrorists. Security, on the ground and in the air, has been increased since 9/11.

aimed at strengthening its ability to prevent such attacks, but these reform efforts failed to implement organization-wide institutional change.

There were opportunities for intelligence and law enforcement to exploit al Qaeda's travel vulnerabilities. Considered collectively, the 9/11 hijackers included known al Qaeda operatives who could have been watchlisted;

• presented passports manipulated in a fraudulent manner;

• presented passports with suspicious indicators of extremism;

• made detectable false statements on visa applications;

• made false statements to border officials to gain entry into the United States; and

• violated immigration laws while in the United States.

Neither the State Department's consular officers nor the Immigration and Naturalization Service's inspectors and agents were ever considered full partners in a national counterterrorism effort. Protecting borders was not a national security issue before 9/11.

Permeable Aviation Security

Hijackers studied publicly available materials on the aviation security system and used items that had less metal content than a handgun and were most likely permissible. Though two of the hijackers were on the U.S. TIPOFF terrorist watchlist, the FAA did not use TIPOFF data. The hijackers had to beat only one layer of secu-

The hijackers had to beat only one layer of security

rity – the security checkpoint process. Even though several hijackers were selected for extra screening by the CAPPS system, this led only to greater scrutiny of their checked baggage. Once on board, the hijackers were faced with aircraft personnel who were trained to be nonconfrontational in the event of a hijacking.

Financing

The 9/11 attacks cost somewhere between $400,000 and $500,000 to execute. The operatives spent more than $270,000 in the United States.

The conspiracy made extensive use of banks in the United States. To date, we have not been able to determine the origin of the money used for the 9/11 attacks. Al Qaeda had many sources of funding and a pre-9/11 annual budget estimated at $30 million.

An Improvised Homeland Defense

The civilian and military defenders of the nation's airspace – FAA and NORAD – were unprepared for the attacks launched against them. Given that lack of preparedness, they attempted and failed to improvise an effective homeland defense against an unprecedented challenge.

The events of that morning do not reflect discredit on operational personnel. NORAD's Northeast Air Defense Sector personnel

U.S. Secretary of Homeland Security, Tom Ridge, is responsible
for protecting the country against future terrorist attacks.

reached out for information and made the best judgments they could based on the information they received. Individual FAA controllers, facility managers, and command center managers were creative and agile in recommending a nationwide alert, ground-stopping local traffic, ordering all aircraft nationwide to land, and executing that unprecedented order flawlessly.

Military Disorganization

At more senior levels, communication was poor. Senior military and FAA leaders had no effective communication with each other. The chain of command did not function well. The President could not reach some senior officials. The Secretary of Defense did not enter the chain of command until the morning's key events were over. Air National Guard units with different rules of engagement were scrambled without the knowledge of the President, NORAD, or the National Military Command Center.

Emergency Response

The civilians, firefighters, police officers, emergency medical technicians, and emergency management professionals exhibited steady determination and resolve under horrifying, overwhelming conditions on 9/11. Their actions saved lives and inspired a nation.

Are We Safer?

Since 9/11, the United States and its allies have killed or captured a majority of al Qaeda's leadership; toppled the Taliban, which gave al Qaeda sanctuary in Afghanistan; and severely damaged the organization. Yet terrorist attacks continue. Even as we have thwarted attacks, nearly everyone expects they will come.

How can this be? The problem is that al Qaeda represents an ideological movement, not a finite group of people. It initiates and inspires, even if it no longer directs. In this way it has transformed itself into a decentralized force. Bin Ladin may be limited in his ability to organize major attacks from his hideouts. Yet killing or capturing him, while extremely important, would not end terror. His message of inspiration to a new generation of terrorists would continue.

Because of offensive actions against al Qaeda since 9/11, and defensive actions to improve homeland security, we believe we are safer today. But we are not safe. We therefore make the following recommendations that we believe can make America safer and more secure.

The emergency service crews in New York City earned the praise and thanks of millions on 9/11 for their bravery and dedication.

Recommendations

Three years after 9/11, the national debate continues about how to protect our nation in this new era. The enemy is not just "terrorism." It is the threat posed specifically by Islamist terrorism, by Bin Ladin and others who draw on a long tradition of extreme intolerance within a minority strain of Islam that does not distinguish politics from religion, and distorts both.

The enemy is not Islam, the great world faith, but a perversion of Islam. The enemy goes beyond al Qaeda to include the radical ideological movement, inspired in part by al Qaeda, that has spawned other terrorist groups and violence.

The first phase of our post-9/11 efforts rightly included military action to topple the Taliban and pursue al Qaeda. This work continues. But long-term success demands the use of all elements of national power: diplomacy, intelligence, covert action, law enforcement, economic policy, foreign aid, public diplomacy, and homeland defense. If we favor one tool while neglecting others, we leave ourselves vulnerable and weaken our national effort.

A symbol of tyranny topples in Iraq

What should Americans expect from their government? The goal seems unlimited: Defeat terrorism anywhere in the world. But Americans have also been told to expect the worst: An attack is probably coming; it may be more devastating still.

Al Qaeda and other groups are popularly described as being all over the world, adaptable, resilient, needing little higher-level organization, and capable of anything. That image lowers expectations of government effectiveness.

It lowers them too far. Our report shows a determined and capable group of plotters. Yet the group was fragile and occasionally left vulnerable by the marginal, unstable people often attracted to such causes. The enemy made mistakes. The U.S. government was not able to capitalize on them.

No president can promise that a catastrophic attack like that of 9/11 will not happen again. But the American people are entitled to expect that officials will have realistic objectives, clear guidance, and effective organization. They are entitled to see standards for performance so they can judge, with the help of their elected representatives, whether the objectives are being met.

The strategy we have recommended is elaborate, even as presented here very briefly. To implement it will require a government better organized than the one that exists today, with its national security institutions designed half a century ago to win the Cold War. Americans should not settle for incremental, ad hoc adjustments to a system created a generation ago for a world that no longer exists.

Our detailed recommendations are designed to fit together. Their purpose is clear: to build unity of effort across the U.S. government. As one official now serving on the front lines overseas put it to us: "One fight, one team."

What The United States Should Do

We propose a strategy with three dimensions:
(1) Attack terrorists and their organizations,
(2) Prevent the continued growth of Islamist terrorism, and
(3) Protect against and prepare for terrorist attacks.

An attack is probably coming; it may be more devastating still

Attack Terrorists And Their Organizations

Root out sanctuaries. The U.S. government should identify and prioritize actual or potential terrorist sanctuaries and have realistic country or regional strategies for each, utilizing every element of national power and reaching out to countries that can help us.

Strengthen long-term U.S. and international commitments to the future of Pakistan and Afghanistan.

Confront problems with Saudi Arabia in the open and build a relation-ship beyond oil, a relationship that both sides can defend to their citizens and includes a shared commitment to reform.

Prevent The Continued Growth Of Islamist Terrorism

In October 2003, Secretary of Defense Donald Rumsfeld asked if enough was being done "to fashion a broad integrated plan to stop the next generation of terrorists." As part of such a plan, the U.S. government should Define the message and stand as an example of moral leadership in the world. To Muslim parents, terrorists like Bin Ladin have nothing to offer their children but visions of violence and death. America and its friends have the advantage – our vision can offer a better future.

• Where Muslim governments, even those

who are friends, do not offer opportunity, respect the rule of law, or tolerate differences, then the United States needs to stand for a better future.

• Communicate and defend American ideals in the Islamic world, through much stronger public diplomacy to reach more people, including students and leaders outside of government. Our efforts here should be as strong as they were in combating closed societies during the Cold War.

• Offer an agenda of opportunity that includes support for public education and economic openness.

• Develop a comprehensive coalition strategy against Islamist terrorism, using a flexible contact group of leading coalition governments and fashioning a common coalition approach on issues like the treatment of captured terrorists.

• Devote a maximum effort to the parallel task of countering the proliferation of weapons of mass destruction.

• Expect less from trying to dry up terrorist money and more from following the money for intelligence, as a tool to hunt terrorists, understand their networks, and disrupt their operations.

Protect Against And Prepare For Terrorist Attacks

• Target terrorist travel, an intelligence and

Our vision can offer a better future

security strategy that the 9/11 story showed could be at least as powerful as the effort devoted to terrorist finance.

• Address problems of screening people with biometric identifiers across agencies and governments, including our border and transportation systems, by designing a comprehensive screening system that addresses common problems and sets common standards. As standards spread, this necessary and ambitious effort could dramatically strengthen the world's ability to intercept individuals who could pose catastrophic threats.

• Quickly complete a biometric entry-exit screening system, one that also speeds qualified travelers.

• Set standards for the issuance of birth certificates and sources of identification, such as driver's licenses.

• Develop strategies for neglected parts of our transportation security system. Since 9/11, about 90 percent of the nation's $5 billion annual investment in transportation security has gone to aviation, to fight the last war.

• In aviation, prevent arguments about a new computerized profiling system from delaying vital improvements in the "no-fly" and "automatic selectee" lists. Also, give priority to the improvement of check-point screening.

• Determine, with leadership from the

President, guidelines for gathering and sharing information in the new security systems that are needed, guidelines that integrate safeguards for privacy and other essential liberties.

• Underscore that as government power necessarily expands in certain ways, the burden of retaining such powers remains on the executive to demonstrate the value of such powers and ensure adequate supervision of how they are used, including a new board to oversee the implementation of the guidelines needed for gathering and sharing information in these new security systems.

The United States must find a way to end the tradition of hatred toward the West.

• Base federal funding for emergency preparedness solely on risks and vulnerabilities, putting New York City and Washington, D.C., at the top of the current list. Such assistance should not remain a program for general revenue sharing or pork-barrel spending.

• Make homeland security funding contingent on the adoption of an incident command system to strengthen teamwork in a crisis, including a regional approach.

• Allocate more radio spectrum and improve connectivity for public safety communications, and encourage wide-spread adoption of newly developed standards for private-sector emergency preparedness – since the private sector controls 85 percent of the nation's critical infrastructure.

Our detailed recommendations are designed to fit together. Their purpose is clear: to build unity of effort across the U.S. government. As one official now serving on the front lines overseas put it to us: "One fight, one team."

We call for unity of effort in five areas, beginning with unity of effort on the challenge of counterterrorism itself:

• unifying strategic intelligence and operational planning against Islamist terrorists across the foreign-domestic divide with a National Counterterrorism Center;

• unifying the intelligence community with a new National Intelligence Director;

• unifying the many participants in the counterterrorism effort and their knowledge in a network-based information sharing system that transcends traditional governmental boundaries;

• unifying and strengthening congressional oversight to improve quality and accountability;

• strengthening the FBI and homeland defenders.

America Rebuilds – Then & Now

The scars on the American landscape were the visible marks every American carried in their hearts after 9/11. The buildings could, and would, be rebuilt. But the lives that were taken could never be replaced.

The New York skyline pre-9/11 was dominated by the elegant lines of the twin towers reaching towards the sky. Today's New York City landscape (inset, right) is a constant visual reminder of what was lost.

America Rebuilds – Then & Now

McDonald's is not only a model of American enterprise, but also of the American spirit. Here, the McDonald's restaurant on lower Broadway on September 11, 2001. At right, only two weeks later, McDonald's is open again for business.

America Rebuilds – Then & Now

Businesses all over New York had to close after the attacks. Giovanni's Atrium, a gourmet Italian restaurant directly across Rector Street from Ground Zero, had to close. But even the terrible devastation couldn't keep the spirit of New York down. Giovanni's Atrium (right) re-opened in only five weeks.

America Rebuilds – Then & Now

Two days after the attack (this page), the rubble of the Twin Towers is still smoldering. At right, ground zero today. Construction is beginning on a World Trade Center memorial.

America Rebuilds – Then & Now

The symbol of America's military might, the Pentagon in Washington, D.C., was seriously wounded in the terrorist attacks. But the hardhats who had the job to rebuild this Fortress of Freedom made the repairs (below) in only one year and showed the world that the spirit of America was alive and well.

The War Against Terror

America's military response to the 9/11 terrorist attacks was swift and overwhelming. On October 7, 2001, three major Afghanistan terrorist sites were attacked and destroyed. By Christmas, the Taliban rulers were on the run.

On March 19, 2003, the first bombs fell on Iraq. By April, Baghdad was a free city. On December 13, 2003, Saddam Hussein was captured, hiding like a coward in a hole in the ground.

The War Against Terror continues today as thousands of American military personnel risk their lives to insure not only the freedom and safety of the United States, but of people everywhere.

A Marine, with an American flag tucked into his jacket, prepares to land in Afghanistan.

Soldiers from the 82nd Airborne Division go door-to-door in Afghanistan searching for Taliban terrorists.

This American flag bears the names of all the New York victims of the 9/11 attacks. It was brought by the Marines to Afghanistan and when Kandahar Airport was captured, they proudly raised the flag as a symbol of freedom and to honor those who died in the attacks.

The statue of Saddam Hussein is toppled by the Iraqi people.

Marine infantry pile out of their armored personnel carrier as the battle in Iraq heats up.

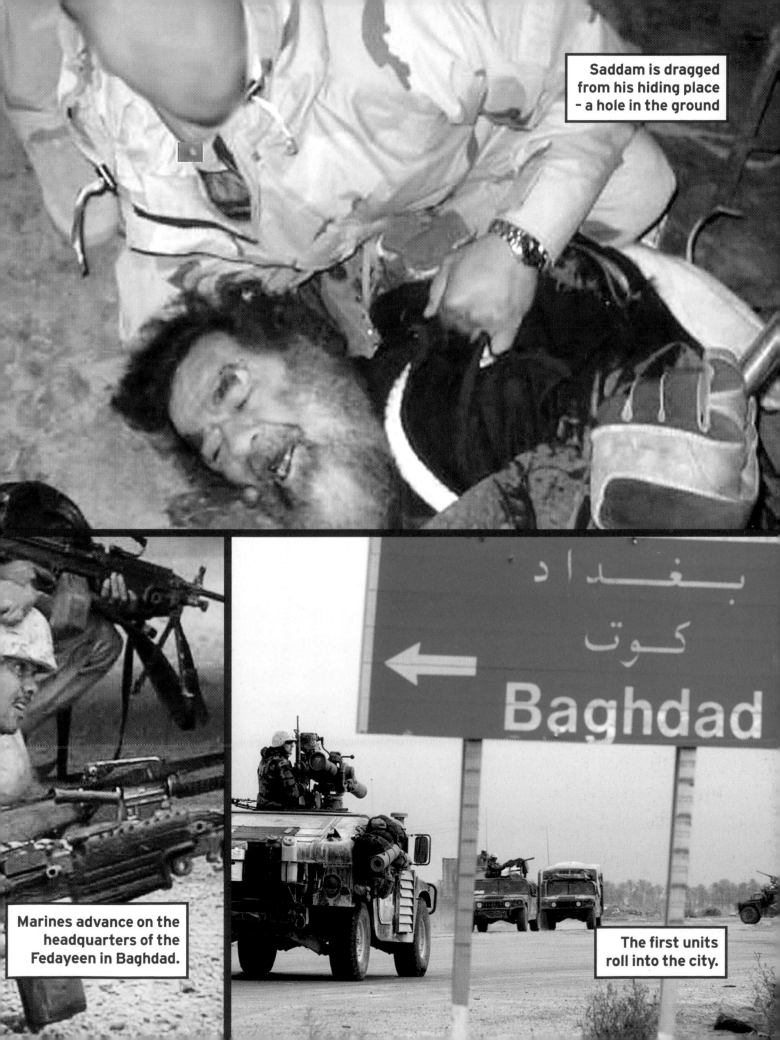

Saddam is dragged from his hiding place - a hole in the ground

Marines advance on the headquarters of the Fedayeen in Baghdad.

بغداد
كوت
Baghdad

The first units roll into the city.

America Remembers

America was united, as never before, in her determination to bring the terrorists to justice, and to honor and respect those who had died at the hands of these criminals. All around the country, the spirit of America burned brighter than ever as everyone - in their own way - memorialized the victims of 9/11 with the whispered promise that we will never forget.

SHANKSVILLE SALUTES 'THE HEROES' OF FLIGHT #93

TERRORIST ATTACKS CAN SHAKE THE FOUNDATIONS OF OUR BIGGEST BUILDINGS, BUT THEY CANNOT TOUCH THE FOUNDATION OF AMERICA.

PRESIDENT GEORGE W. BUSH
SEPTEMBER 11, 2001

TO HONOR AND REMEMBER THOSE WHO LOST THEIR LIVES ON SEPTEMBER 11, 2001 AND AS A TRIBUTE TO THE
ENDURING SPIRIT OF FREEDOM

Your bravery, your lives, will not be forgotten.

Special Edition of The 9/11 Commission Report

EDITOR
David Perel

MANAGING EDITOR
Nancy W. Miller

DESIGN EDITOR
Carlos Plaza

PHOTO EDITOR
Sally Westbrook

DESIGNERS
Preston Pisellini, Erika Rains, Jayme Rans

This book is available in quantity at special discounts for your group or organization. For further information, contact:

Triumph Books
601 S. LaSalle St.
Suite 500
Chicago, Illinois 60605
Phone: (312) 939-3330
Fax: (312) 663-3557

Printed in the United States of America

"We hope that the terrible losses chronicled in this report can create something positive— an America that is safer, stronger, and wiser. That September day, we came together as a nation. The test before us is to sustain that unity of purpose and meet the challenges now confronting us."

– Thomas H. Kean, Chair
Lee H. Hamilton, Vice Chair
9/11 Commission